PERFECT PITCH:

Color Hearing for
Expanded Musical Awareness

The time between the notes relates the color to the scenes. . .

—*Yes*
(Close to the Edge, Atlantic
Recording Corp.)

PERFECT PITCH:

COLOR HEARING FOR EXPANDED MUSICAL AWARENESS

DAVID L. BURGE

ISBN: 0-942542-97-5
Library of Congress Catalog Card No.: 81-85963

Printed in the United States of America.

First Printing: February 1981
Second Printing: February 1983
Third Printing: October 1984
Fourth Printing: December 1985
Fifth Printing: March 1987
Sixth Printing: February 1989
Seventh Printing: May 1992
Eighth Printing: March 1994

The ear-training techniques in this handbook
have been found effective by thousands of
musicians around the world, and by research at
leading educational institutions. Please write the
publisher at the address below for more
information and research summaries.

This work comprises the original teaching
material directly from the author's own hand. It
has not been edited, abridged, or changed in any
manner whatsoever.

Comments on this book may be sent to the
author at the publisher's address. All letters will
be forwarded to Mr. Burge; we regret that it is not
physically possible to respond to each and every
one. Your letters or completed questionnaires are
sincerely appreciated, and all will be personally
read and evaluated by Mr. Burge.

Published by:
American Educational Music Publications, Inc.
Music Resources Building
1106 E. Burlington Avenue, Fairfield, IA 52556
Telephone (515) 472-3100; FAX (515) 472-2700

This composition is dedicated with deepest love and respect to my teacher, Helene Rynd Vinograd, who opened my ears to the color and fascination of music.

A special note of appreciation goes to David J. O'Reilly for his assistance in the preparation of this Course.

Instructions:

Exceptional courses usually have a handbook and a teacher to explain the points in detail. This handbook is required for use with **The Perfect Pitch**® **SuperCourse**™ tapes. Experience has shown that musicians who hear Mr. Burge speak have greater comprehension, clearer experiences, and faster results with their ear-training.

Your Perfect Pitch tapes do not contain drills on them like Burge's **Relative Pitch Ear-Training Course**™ (find out why on tapes). Although Perfect Pitch is very simple, it is extremely delicate. It is a different kind of training which is easy to do, but it requires an artful degree of understanding in order to practice the *Color Hearing Technique Exercises*™ effectively. The purpose of the tapes and this handbook is to give you that skillful understanding.

How to use your Course materials:
Listen first to the **PERFECT PITCH**® **SEMINAR**™ tapes (Workshop Tape 1 and Master Class Tape 2). Then study this simple handbook and work with the exercises. After about three weeks, listen to the **COLOR HEARING "HELP ME" TAPES**™. Produced by Burge after years of experience with students at colleges and universities, the **COLOR HEARING "HELP ME" TAPES**™ answer important questions which commonly arise regarding easy practice technique, pitch color perception, solutions to various "difficulties," and advanced techniques and experiences with *Color Hearing* (Perfect Pitch). **NOTE:** If you should encounter any pressing questions about your Perfect Pitch practice, please listen to the **COLOR HEARING "HELP ME" TAPES**™ immediately, without waiting the three week period.

The latest addition to the SuperCourse is the **Perfect Pitch Solo Tape**™ (tape 5). It contains excellent techniques you can do by yourself to deepen your experience of the Perfect Pitch colors.

Immediate benefits which are regularly reported from this Course include: increased aural alertness, greater musical sensitivity, and finer perception, enjoyment and creativity. Benefits over several months: Correct daily practice of Burge's *Color Hearing Technique*™ directly cultures fully established Perfect Pitch in the fastest way possible, and enhances all aspects of listening and musical aptitude.

Optional tape: **Perfect Pitch for the Young or Beginning Musician**™ (for description, see current *Perfect Pitch Report* from publisher).

Other tapes by David L. Burge: **THE RELATIVE PITCH EAR-TRAINING COURSE**™ —twenty-one 90-minute audio cassette tapes, a total of 41 Lessons plus Introductory Talk. Burge's complete companion course for gaining Relative Pitch—a gold mine of ear-training drills right on tape for you to enjoy. For information, request *Relative Pitch Report* from publisher.

For additional information, call or write: American Educational Music Publications, Inc., Music Resources Building, 1106 E. Burlington Avenue, Fairfield, IA 52556, 24 Hour Telephone: (515) 472-3100; FAX: (515) 472-2700

CONTENTS

I. THERE'S COLOR IN YOUR EAR!

Almost everyone has heard of the supernormal hearing ability called *perfect pitch*. The musician with perfect pitch is a constant source of fascination and wonder for knowing the pitch of any musical tone *by ear alone*. Just as most people can name different colors of thread within a multicolored fabric, the musician with perfect pitch can name the various tones in a piece just by hearing them.

The musician with perfect pitch can tell what a note is without looking at the instrument playing. He or she always knows the keys in which pieces are being played, can discern whether a band is sharp or flat, and can name all the chords to your favorite song as it plays on the radio. The musician with perfect pitch seems to display an expanded perceptual awareness which he can apply to practical musicianship.

Musicians lacking development of perfect pitch generally assume that it is difficult to develop or that one either "has it" or one does not. Many consider perfect pitch a musical "gift" and associate it only with exceptional and prodigious personalities.

Mozart, for example, was particularly noted (among other things) for his highly acute sense of perfect pitch. A story is often told of a time when he was seven years old and a friend lent him a violin he especially liked. Young Wolfgang enjoyed this violin for its pleasing sound, but after playing it for some time he discarded it and sought out his own little one. Later while practicing his own instrument, his friend remarked about this. The child paused in his playing and complained that the other violin had been "half a quarter of a tone flatter" than his own. To have detected this by ear alone without direct comparison of the two instruments seemed ridiculous. Even so, his father insisted that both violins be brought forth to test the boy's accuracy, which of course proved impeccable. (Why young Wolfgang didn't simply retune the violin is not included in the account, the main point being that, even at an early age, Mozart was recognized as possessing an exceptional musical ear.)[1]

Due to such connotations surrounding the subject of perfect pitch, many musicians feel an impossibility of ever enjoying this proficiency. Actually, this super-refinement of hearing is not a mystical gift of pitch bestowed only on the musical elect. The ear of every musician has a natural, but usually undeveloped ability to discern "color" within the pitch spectrum, much as the eye sees "color" within the visible spectrum. There are scores of musicians today who have developed perfect pitch and the proficiencies which go along with it. Perfect pitch is *color hearing*—a refined perception of "color" within the *sound* spectrum—and it can be easily "learned" by most people when they know *how* to listen.

You can easily prove your own latent ability to acquire perfect pitch. Go to a piano that is fairly well tuned and listen to both the Eb and F# below Middle C. Do you notice that the F# seems to have some sort of a "twangy," "vibrant" quality, whereas the Eb seems "softer," more "mellow"? When this is pointed out, most people are immediately surprised that they *do* seem to hear this distinction, but had never listened closely enough to discover it before. It is this "twanginess," "softness," or other quality of a pitch which is its characteristic *color*.

The "twangy" color of F# might be compared to the visual color of red. The bold vibrancy of red seems to "stick out" more than other visual colors, which is why red is often used for flags, warnings, etc. In a similar way, F# seems to "stick out" above all other pitches because of its bold "color." For most musicians, F# is the easiest pitch color to notice.

Some musicians can immediately hear this "twangy" color of F# so well that they insist there must be something about their particular piano which causes this. However, F# sounds the same way on *any* piano which is in tune! Tones of the same pitch always have the same pitch color, regardless of the instrument playing.

The undeveloped ear can usually hear pitch color best on the piano at first, probably due to some extent to the large sounding board which seems to help clarify the color of the pitch. An amplified electric guitar also seems to make the "vibrant" pitch color of F# or "mellow" color of Eb more noticeable to the undeveloped ear. However, you may find that at first pitch color is only noticeable on your familiar instrument, whatever that may be.

A musician with developed perfect pitch simply has his ears fully open to these fine qualities of pitch color as they are perceived through the various textures of many different musical instruments. If you can clearly hear the colors on the piano as indicated above, but cannot hear them on another instrument, or if you are not certain even on the piano, do not despair. Rather than a facility which one either "has" or "does not have," perfect pitch in reality is an expanded musical awareness which can be easily cultured by certain "ear opening" exercises.

Color hearing may at first seem very abstract, but once your ear catches onto it, a whole new field of musical experience will become apparent.

II. THE IMPORTANCE OF COLOR HEARING

Musicians commonly define perfect pitch (technically known as *absolute pitch*) as the ability to name any tone heard and sing any note requested. There are many reasons for cultivating this inborn yet usually undeveloped musical perception.

Of the many facets to superior musicianship, a good ear is the essential foundation. A good sense of pitch is considered by professional musicians to be the most valuable element of musicianship, and is even chosen above other essentials like good rhythm, technical facility, accurate memory, intensity discrimination and creativity.[2] Perfect pitch can be a master key to fluent improvisation and playing by ear. Perfect pitch is also a stable basis for confidence during performance. Memorization is made much more secure when the ear hears in terms of color patterns *in addition* to finger memory and theoretical familiarity with a piece.

Singers find perfect pitch an invaluable aid for locating obscure pitches in precarious situations. A brilliant effect can be produced when a singer arrives onstage and does not require a starting pitch. After singing briefly the instrumentalists join in, and—to the delight of the audience—everyone is together in tune.

These kinds of proficiencies are in themselves often considered as the ability of perfect pitch, but really they are all skills which are rooted in the one basic ability to perceive pitch color. Yet even if a musician would not apply his sense of color hearing to practical musicianship, there is a higher aesthetic appreciation of sound which dawns in his refined ear.

Imagine the most glorious sights your eyes have witnessed in life: color-splashed sunsets, the iridescent hues of spring, summer and autumn, all the majestic artistry of nature. Now think how you would describe these sights to someone who sees, but who does not recognize visual color. Total color-blindness is extremely rare, but 8% of all men (less than .5% of women) have some degree of visual color perception disability and confuse obviously different hues like red and green. If you are not one of these people, imagine *not* clearly seeing the difference between the red of a rose and the green of its leaf! The

11

inhibition of artistic appreciation in life can hardly be compensated for! Yet the musician lacking aural development unknowingly finds himself in a similar sort of situation.

To the *color ear,* the entire pitch spectrum is a dazzling display of distinct sound colors which dance within their musical framework and blend in various ways to form the different chords and tonalities. Acoustical psychologist A. Bachem has observed that "particular characteristics of certain keys, e.g., the brilliancy of A major, the softness of D flat major, can only be appreciated fully through absolute pitch."[3] In addition, the color ear experiences a certain richness of sound which extends even beyond the musical sphere.

By comparison, the ear that has not penetrated to this depth of experience lives in a shadow musical world "painted" only in shades of "grey" pitches which, though individually distinct, are somehow all the same. The common musical ear certainly has no trouble hearing pitches and can certainly enjoy all forms of music, but it is inhibited in its scope because it does not recognize the subtle value of *color*—that quality which distinguishes a pitch in its own right, without comparison to other tones.

This is unfortunate because, unlike visual color-blindness, there is nothing inherently "wrong" with most ears that would prevent full pitch color awareness. The chief reason why people, including musicians, have an undeveloped sense of color hearing (apparent "color-deafness") is largely lack of aural orientation in life.

Psychologists differ as to the extent each sense contributes to our total perceptual scope, but many feel we are about 80-90% *visually* oriented. Early in life we are taught the names of *visual* colors, but seldom does a child learn the *musical* colors of F#, Bb, etc. Our vision is almost a necessity of everyday life and has certainly become our dominant sense. If you stop to think about it, it becomes apparent that we use our eyes for almost everything we do— except, of course, for listening to music. In fact, about the hardest thing our *ears* have had to deal with until musical development is the differences between spoken words. Imagine how developed our hearing would be if we had spent as much time in school listening to sounds and music as we did in reading and writing, science and mathematics!

As a result of a one-sided attention favoring the sense of sight, most ears are still "sleeping" to greater possibilities of experience and are not fully enlivened to more abstract values of sound. It is as if the ear has taken on some dullness or laziness because it has never really had to listen intently. The so-called "tone deaf" individual is largely a myth. Most people labelled as tone deaf appear so only due to lack of musical development rather than to any real disability in hearing pitches.

For most individuals, hearing is therefore a more elusive sense than sight. Because color hearing is an even subtler experience than grosser sound perception, it is easy to see how the sense of perfect pitch is obscured from awareness. Yet the ear has always been *capable* of hearing pitch color. Most musicians, in fact, are already hearing pitch color to some extent, but because they are not consciously aware of it, they do not fully appreciate it. Because most ears have never really *related* to color, color hearing has remained an untapped and little understood possibility.

As the art of coherent sound, music deals exclusively with acoustic vibrations as interpreted through our sense of hearing. Our scope of musical comprehension is therefore limited only by our boundaries of aural awareness. By increasing one's sensitivity to musical tones, one not only enlivens his appreciation of musical art, but also instills into his awareness an intuitive cognition of the finer mechanics of this art.

The apparatus of the ear is already latent with the ability to discern pitch color, so no new faculty of hearing needs to be created—one needs only to become *attentive* to a level of musical experience which previously went unnoticed. The key to acquiring a sense of color hearing lies only in expanding one's restricted musical awareness by learning how to listen in a more refined and natural manner. In cultivating perfect pitch, one's aural perception becomes increasingly broadened and alert, thereby forming a more comprehensive basis which facilitates all avenues of musicality. Expanded musical awareness is both cause and effect of acquiring this phenomenal mastery of musical frequencies.

III. WAVE FREQUENCY AND COLOR

The mechanics of perfect pitch are quite simple and can be understood by comparing the sense of hearing with the sense of sight. Let's look at some facts and figures on visual and aural perception and then make an analogy between them.

Both visual and aural sensory fields relate to *wave frequencies*. The frequency of a sound or light wave means its number of *vibrations per second* (or *cycles per second*). This is expressed in *hertz* (Hz), one hertz meaning one cycle per second.

The eye can see light wave frequencies from about 4.5×10^{14} Hz to about 7.8×10^{14} Hz, and somehow perceives them as a distinct prismatic color spectrum: red, orange, yellow, green, blue, indigo, violet—with all the hues in between.

The ear is sensitive to a comparatively larger range of sound wave frequencies from approximately 16 Hz to about 20,000 Hz (some people can hear as high as 30,000-40,000 Hz). Within this continuous pitch spectrum, Western music today uses about 88 specific pitches (each has its own "color"), as can be seen on a piano keyboard. Contemporary *concert pitch* is set at A-440, which means that the accepted standard of pitch is such that the A above Middle C is set at a frequency of 440 vibrations per second (or 440 Hz) and thus sets all other tones accordingly. Each successive octave on the keyboard is *twice* the frequency of the previous one, and each octave is divided up into twelve *semitones,* or chromatic degrees.

With this information and a little math, it can be shown that the frequency of any tone times the twelfth root of two (which equals about 1.0595) will equal the frequency of the next higher tone (i.e., A-440 $\times$ 1.0595 = Bb-466, the next chromatic degree higher). Thus we can calculate that the lowest tone on the piano is A-27.5 and the highest tone is C-4186 (Middle C has a frequency of 261.7 Hz), each tone lying well within the ear's limits.

Again considering that each octave higher is twice the frequency of the previous octave, it becomes apparent that the ear has a complete hearing range of ten to eleven octaves, compared to less than one for visual perception. The

14

ear, therefore, within its own field, seems to contain more perceptual possibilities than even the eye. In fact, the ear is such a delicate and perfect instrument of perception that it is easy to understand how it could also possess a natural ability to appreciate different wave frequencies (pitches) as different "colors" within the *sound* spectrum, just as in the visual field the eye naturally sees all the colors of the rainbow according to their appointed frequencies.

Every pitch we hear has a particular wave frequency, and because of this every pitch has a particular sound color. All we need to do to hear these colors is simply *learn to listen.*

****

Many musicians have already developed a color ear. But what exactly is such an individual's experience? It is easy to understand color in terms of sight, but when applied to the sense of hearing, the word *color* may carry connotations which do not necessarily belong to the sense of perfect pitch.

Let us at this point clarify exactly what is meant when we talk in terms of *color hearing,* the ability to hear "pitch color" within the sound spectrum. To avoid foreseeable confusion, we will examine related topics to make a distinction between them and color hearing.

IV. COLOR HEARING AND TIMBRE

Musicians often use the term *tone color* when referring to the characteristic quality of a tone which enables one to tell different instruments apart. "Tone color," or *timbre* (pronounced "tam-ber"), is the characteristic pattern of overtones unique to every instrument which gives an instrument its own distinct sound. If you play a tone on a trumpet, then another on an oboe, it is easy to tell which instrument is which by its quality of timbre. Timbre is what gives a tone its "brassy," "reedy," "stringy," "hollow," "rich," etc. sound.

The overtones which produce the quality of timbre are much weaker than the fundamental tone sounded, so they usually are not consciously noticed by the musician. But if you listen carefully it is not hard to hear many of them.

Go to a piano and play the C two below Middle C. A string vibrates not only as one long string length, but also in halves, thirds, fourths, *ad infinitum,* and therefore corresponding overtones are produced which can be heard. By multiplying the frequency of the fundamental tone by two, three, four, etc., we can calculate the frequencies of its overtones. With this particular C sounding, the pitches shown in Figure 1 are also sounding, many of which can be heard if you listen very closely.

Try this experiment: Depress Middle C, but do not allow it to sound. Next play Low C, but only let it sound briefly. You will notice that Middle C is now sounding. The first overtone of Low C is identical in pitch to Middle C and thus causes the Middle C strings to sympathetically vibrate. Try this with Low C and Middle C#. It will not work because Middle C# is not an overtone of Low C. Nor can Middle C cause Low C to vibrate (it can, however, cause Low C's *overtone* to sound!). You can repeat this experiment with other overtones, but they will not all work due to mathematical differences of pitch between natural harmonic overtones and the actual contemporary Western twelve tone scale.

It is the presence, absence, and relative strength of overtones and where they occur in the harmonic structure which determines the "tone color," or timbre of an instrument. Figure 2 shows a sound wave graph which represents a pure tone from a tuning fork, which essentially does not have any overtones, or timbre. The pattern of a tuning fork sound wave is just a simple sine wave. The overtone series unique to a musical instrument shows up on a sound wave graph as fluctuations within this basic sine wave pattern, as shown in Figure

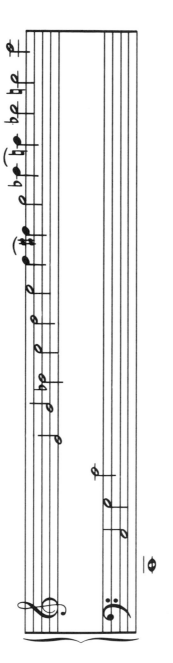

Figure 1: FIRST 15 OVERTONES OF C

Figure 2: PURE SINE WAVE

Sound wave graph pattern of a tuning fork, which essentially has no overtones.

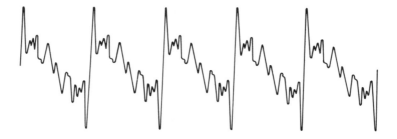

Figure 3: COMPOSITE WAVE

Sound wave graph pattern of a fundamental tone with overtones. Overtones show up as fluctuations in the basic sine wave pattern, and register in the ear as the *timbre*, or sound quality of the instrument.

3. Every musical instrument has a different wave pattern produced by its characteristic arrangement of overtones which registers in our ear as its timbre, or unique sound of the instrument.

Though musicians universally refer to the quality of timbre as "tone color," it is really a misnomer. Qualities like "brassy," "reedy," "stringy," etc. are not *colors*—they are more like *textures*. If something sounds "brassy," for instance, that is really a textural quality rather than a kind of aural *color*.

Because musicians are inherently poetic at heart, it is pleasing to employ such a lyrical word as *color* in music vocabulary and even use it liberally in other respects as well. In addition to "tone color," we also speak of "color" with reference to harmonic texture, melodic disposition, dynamics, register, ornamental and interpretive devices, as well as the general character of a work. *Color* means a unit of melodic repetition when referring to French *Ars Nova* forms of music of the fourteenth century. All these usages are really free interpretations of a word which also has a specific meaning in physics: the perceived quality of a wave frequency which allows one to recognize that wave frequency on the basis of perception alone. Because *pitch color* means *the unique sound of a wave frequency,* it is a more accurate usage of the word *color* than any of those previously mentioned.

As stated earlier, the *textural* form a pitch takes (its timbre) can be represented by its particular graph pattern, as shown in Figure 3. On the other hand, what determines *pitch color* (as contrasted with timbre) is *how many* of these waves are produced per second, as we discussed when comparing the sense of hearing to the sense of sight. The more waves per second (Hz), the higher the pitch will be, and each pitch has a different color sound.

The graph pattern of a particular instrument is its "fingerprint" of timbre. No matter what pitch is sounding, the graph pattern will have the same basic design which represents the texture of that particular instrument. The *colors* of concert pitches, however, are the same on *all* instruments when compared to the *same pitches* (frequencies), but these colors wear the disguise of many different "tone textures" according to the instrument sounding. With this understanding it is easy to analyze the mechanics of tonal discrimination in the developed ear: if a Bb is sounded on a flute, one knows it is a Bb by hearing its *color* (pitch color discrimination), and one knows it is a flute by its sweet, hollow sounding *texture* (timbre discrimination).

The point here is to make the distinction between "tone color" (which is really tone *texture)* and other general usages of the word *color,* and color hearing, which is the ear's perception of pitch color. It may have been agreeable not to have added another definition of *color* to the musician's already crowded list, but the sense of perfect pitch is master of this word and therefore rightfully deserves its place.

V. COLOR HEARING AND SYNESTHESIA

Some people have a perception of musical tones which extends beyond the sense of hearing and "overflows" into other senses, particularly the sense of sight. That is, when they hear a musical tone they may simultaneously see an actual *visual* color. This extremely rare and peculiar phenomenon is called *synesthesia,* which means that one of the five senses is stimulated through a different sense outside its own field of perception. The synesthetic individual literally "sees" a color when he hears a tone.

This situation has no direct connection with the ability of perfect pitch. A person with perfect pitch does not *see* a *visual color* when he hears a tone; rather, he *hears* the *sound color* (pitch color) of the tone. Visual color and pitch color can both be referred to as color because they both mean a certain quality which allows one to discriminate among wave frequencies.

If this seems to be an abstract conception when applied to the sense of hearing, it appears so only due to unfamiliarity with pitch color perception. If you were to try to explain how different frequencies of light appear to your eyes as "red," "orange," "blue," etc., you may find that intelligent descriptions elude you even though what you see is perfectly obvious to your perception. But the proof that you *do* see color is the fact that you can identify specific bands of light frequencies just by how they appear to your eye.

In a similar manner, it can be difficult to explain how the musical pitch spectrum is perceived as various "colors" which are *heard.* Even most people with perfect pitch can not explain how they perceive the difference between tones. If played a C#, color hearers will know it is a C# by ear alone. But if asked *how* they know this, most will say something like, "I don't know—it just *sounds* like a C#." Color, whether visual or aural, is difficult to convey to someone who does not have that experience.

Each tone on any musical instrument is a different wave frequency, however, and therefore should be *heard* as a different "color": C, C#, D, Eb, etc. If you hear a C# and do not know it is a C# rather than a Bb, you have not as yet become aware of the *color* of C#.

The proof that someone with perfect pitch does hear colors of pitch is the fact that he or she can identify specific bands of frequencies (musical pitches) just by how they sound to his ear. If one is color-blind or "color-deaf," one will not be able to consistently identify visual or aural colors. It is not that one as such perceives *nothing*—a color-blind individual at worst still sees shades of grey light, and the (apparently) "color-deaf" individual still hears gradations of pitch. It just means that perceptual awareness is not yet complete. Unless a careful *comparison* of the perception is made with a specific given standard, there will be difficulty in identifying the name of the color frequency. *Color discrimination,* whether visual or aural, simply gives the unique perception of a wave frequency which allows you to identify it *without reference to anything else*—i.e., red always basically appears as red, F# always sounds like F#, and it is not necessary to refer to any other perception to know this.

The point of this section is that color exists both in the fields of sight *and* hearing. It is important to note that it is not our goal here to indicate a strict and definite correlation of the two senses, which could prove to be a difficult task, but rather to show by analogy that wave frequencies can be *heard* as colors within the sound spectrum much the same as they are *seen* as colors within the visual spectrum. Further, individuals with the sense of color hearing (perfect pitch) do not *see* colors when tones are played (this is synesthesia), but rather discriminate between colors which are *heard.*

VI. COLOR HEARING AND COLOR ASSOCIATION

Since the dawn of musical history, man has associated visual colors with various functions in music, such as individual notes, tonality, tempo, scale degree, register, timbre, harmonic texture, as well as individual compositions and the entire works of some composers. Ancient philosophy of India relates the degrees of the scale *(do, re, mi, fa, sol, la, ti)* to the colors green, red, gold, yellowish-white, black, yellow and a combination of all colors for the seventh diatonic degree.[4] In the fourth century B.C. Aristotle pondered on a relationship between visual color and music in his *De Sensu.* In the seventeenth century Sir Isaac Newton went so far as to mathematically correlate the prismatic colors red through violet with the scale tones C, D, Eb, F, G, A, and Bb respectively[5] (a C scale in the Dorian mode). Beethoven, Liszt, Schubert, Scriabin, Rimsky-Korsakoff, MacDowell and other composers have been known to express direct associations of musical tones and/or key tonalities with visual color. The impressionistic "paintings" of Claude Debussy are fantastic works of musical color which seem to reveal the composer's conscious efforts in this regard.

In his book *Color Psychology and Color Therapy,* Faber Birren has noted that:

> Among other composers Liszt is credited with several pet phrases: "More pink here." "This is too black." "I want it all azure." Beethoven called B minor the black key. Schubert likened E minor "unto a maiden robed in white and with a rose-red bow on her breast." To Rimsky-Korsakoff sunlight was C major, and F# was strawberry red.[6]

There is a fine distinction between color association and true synesthesia. Whereas synesthesia is actually "seeing" a color upon hearing a tone, color association is a purely psychological connection between the name of a note (or some other factor of music) and a visual color. For example, many musicians feel an association of color to various musical tonalities. However, most of these musicians are not able to identify these keys by the colors they allegedly "sound like." Thus it becomes obvious that such associations of color are not based on a kind of constant synesthetic experience, but rather on purely subjective psychological considerations.

Also, it is hard to say whether the above composers were "seeing" color (synesthesia) or associating visual color to pitch color, as probably all could be consistent in their color schemes due to perfect pitch. When Beethoven referred to B minor as the "black" key, he certainly could pick this key out by ear from any other key due to perfect pitch. Whether he heard it *synesthetically* as "black" each time or whether he *associated* black to what he knew was B minor is something we do not know. (In any event, Beethoven's "black" B minor is about equivalent to today's Bb minor due to the rise of pitch standards.)

On the whole, there seems to be little correlation between different individuals' musical color associations. It is interesting to note that none of the composers mentioned associated visual colors to music in precisely the same way as another. For instance, Scriabin labelled A major as a "yellow" key, whereas Rimsky-Korsakoff felt it to be rose-colored.[7]

Of the many psychological considerations affecting color association, the musical terms *sharp* and *flat* seem to connote "brightness" and "somberness" in our minds as they do when used in other non-musical contexts. For this reason, F#, for example, is more often associated to a bright color, while Gb, *the same pitch,* is more often thought of as a darker hue.

In conclusion we can state that, whether synesthesia or color association, one's correlation of music to visual color can be extremely subjective. Yet for perhaps this very reason relationships connecting visual color and music persist, and people seem to feel an irresistible and mystical unity between the senses of sight and hearing. Even the languages of the musician and artist are replete with related expressions as we all talk in terms of color, tone, chromatics, pitch, shading, brightness, intensity, volume, etc. One of the earliest references to a formal coordination of the two arts was by Louis Bertrand Castel in his *La Musique en Couleurs* (1720). The art of color music has since had many innovations and pioneers. Russian composer Alexander Scriabin scored a colored light fantasia to accompany his *Promethius, the Poem of Fire* (1910). Arthur Bliss created an entire symphony with each movement named after a color. And of course, the light show at many concerts today is another variation on this same theme.

It should be clear by this analysis that color hearing (perfect pitch) is completely separate from any kind of visual color association to music. Color association simply means various connotations of visual color imposed upon various musical functions. Perfect pitch, on the other hand, is the *perception of pitch color* and has no concern with any kind of visual color experience or association. Pitch color is a quality which is *heard* and is merely analogous to the way the eye sees and discriminates between visual colors.

(Note: Even though color hearing and color association are distinctly separate considerations, there can be a value in temporarily "listening" for visual colors as a first step in the culture of perfect pitch, as we will see in the Color Hearing Technique exercises to come.)

VII. PERFECT PITCH AND RELATIVE PITCH

At some point or another every musician encounters the challenge of developing his ear. Students majoring in music usually go through at least two to four years or more of formal music theory/ear-training classes. The self-taught teenage guitarist also practices to become adept at picking up material by ear. The proficiency usually being cultured by these efforts is called *relative pitch.*

Relative pitch is the ability to quickly *compare* the pitches of two tones to determine their distance apart, or *interval.* Music theory classifies the space between two notes as a specific interval relationship, as shown in Figure 4 on the following page. This diagram describes intervals only between C and the note indicated, but the entire scheme can be transposed to any note.

Notice that the *name* of an interval is dependent on how the notes are *spelled* (i.e., F# or Gb), but that the actual *distance* between notes can be the same. For example, F# is *enharmonic* (identical in pitch) with Gb because it is really another spelling of the same tone, so even though we say theoretically that F# is an augmented fourth up from C and Gb is a diminished fifth up from C, the actual distance from C is the same for each.

Relative pitch deals with *relationships.* A musician with relative pitch has become so familiar with all of these intervals that he or she can evaluate relationships between chords and single tones. If played an A and a C#, he can tell you that they comprise an interval of a major third. Or, given an A, he will be able to sing a C# by locating the distance of a major third.

When first developing relative pitch, musicians usually make use of mnemonic devices which aid in remembering what each interval sounds like. A familiar song can be used which contains a particular interval and which helps to remember that interval later. The first two notes of "My Bonnie Lies Over the Ocean" comprise a major sixth, and the second and third tones of "Taps" is a perfect fourth. A good exercise is to think of a song that fits each interval. Then when that interval is heard it can be related to the song and thus to the name of the interval.

The most difficult interval to learn to sing is the augmented fourth, the so-

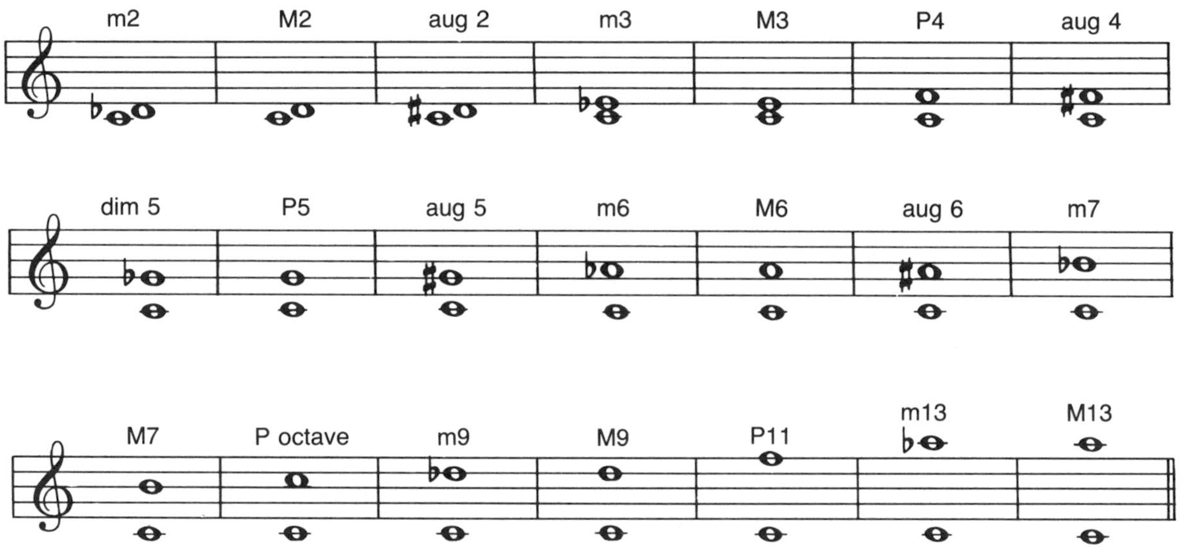

m	=	minor
M	=	major
P	=	perfect
dim	=	diminished
aug	=	augmented

Figure 4: COMMON INTERVALS

called "devil in music" which was strictly taboo in early Christian chant. The augmented fourth can also be called a diminished fifth or *tritone*, the latter name because it is an interval of three whole tones. Master this sound well so it will not deceive you!

Musicians who are first learning relative pitch sometimes complain they cannot think of a piece or song with an obvious tritone sound. Actually, if you listen closely you will find that this interval is an integral part of music from the Baroque period to the present, and is often especially noticeable in modern works and movie and TV scores. In the soundtrack of the *Star Wars* series there is a short recurring melodic phrase whose first and last tones comprise an augmented fourth. Also, the harmonic structure often battles with major chords at a tritone.

Many musicians mistakenly think that good relative pitch is "not quite perfected" perfect pitch, that is, that good relative pitch is a fair *degree* of perfect pitch. Through our analysis it should be clear that relative pitch and perfect pitch are *completely separate functions* of aural perception. Relative pitch means *the ability to evaluate relationships between separate tones,* whereas perfect pitch means *the ability to perceive the pitch color of individual tones.*

Relative pitch is a sort of "horizontal" listening experience. In developing the ability to recognize relationships between tones, relative pitch examines the surface level of aural perception in order to acquire judgment on that level. Perfect pitch is more like "vertical" listening—it penetrates deep *within* the sound of individual tones to a delicate level of experience unnoticed by most ears. Opening the ear to perception of pitch color is in essence an *expansion* of musical awareness (i.e., appreciation of finer values of sound than before), as contrasted with the *focus* of awareness which relative pitch training demands (i.e., learning to compare sounds on the concrete level of perception which is already clear to one's awareness).

For the fully developed musical ear, both perfect pitch and relative pitch must be lively; one cannot replace the other. Both facilities play unique and valuable roles in musical experience, and in their developed forms both augment one's musical expertise from their own levels.

Some musicians with undeveloped color hearing argue that relative pitch is all that is necessary, and in fact say that they would not even desire such "perfect" perception lest they become "too sensitive" to slight yet inevitable tuning discrepancies. This reasoning of course is unfounded, and more often than not exposes such a musician's frustration and lack of understanding of how to develop perfect pitch. Those who have tried unsuccessfully to develop perfect pitch should know that color hearing cannot be gained by any amount of relative pitch training. Color hearing will only evolve after one starts listening for *color.* Many attempts to gain perfect pitch have also failed because musicians have tried to "memorize" a pitch without becoming sensitive to its color. A pitch will not stick permanently in the mind unless there is some quality the mind perceives about it which distinguishes it from other pitches, and that quality is its *color.* Also, the color hearer does not "suffer" due to "too good" an ear—he accepts tuning inconsistencies as would any other musician.

Another kind of argument "against" perfect pitch is implied by a purported incident where a well-known performer was required to transpose a score at sight due to orchestral considerations, and in so doing became embarrassingly confused because the music "sounded all wrong" in the new key. If such a situation like this has arisen, it can only be due to the musician's lack of transposition skills or adequate *relative pitch* development. This therefore is not an argument against perfect pitch, but rather *for relative pitch.*

The New Grove Dictionary of Music and Musicians (1980, Macmillan Publishers Limited) comments on these kinds of misunderstandings concerning perfect pitch:

> Arguments that absolute pitch is of doubtful value to a musician (particularly one engaged in transposition) strike one as if a majority of colour-blind people were to tell a minority of normally sighted ones that, even if they wished to be painters, colour vision is more trouble than it is worth. In fact it is less surprising that the few possess it than that the many are without it.[8]

Development of perfect pitch alone is actually more desirable than relative pitch alone. Even a slight sense of perfect pitch captures a broader territory than fully developed relative pitch, which is why color hearers can usually long outwit the most difficult ear-training drills even without formal relative pitch training. The musician with perfect pitch in fact almost always develops relative pitch spontaneously or with little effort. Because the color ear is wide awake, it does not experience the difficulty of comparing tones which is common among many music students in ear-training classes today.

The color ear hears music from a deeper level than can be realized through relative pitch training. Whereas relative pitch reveals knowledge of musical structure, perfect pitch presents the subtle perception of absolute pitch itself. The sense of perfect pitch admits to the ear consciousness of the *color* in music, the intrinsic artistry of pure sound which is distinct from—yet part of—the actual fabric of music composition.

Both perfect pitch and relative pitch have their own range, however, and for this reason complement each other in an integrated musical experience. Perfect pitch without relative pitch lacks theoretical knowledge of relationships and cannot be fully musically creative. Relative pitch without perfect pitch lacks a deep perception of sound itself and cannot be fully creative or artistically appreciative. But to the fully developed musical ear, relative pitch reveals the framework in which the building blocks of pitch color are arranged. In this way, when perfect pitch and relative pitch are both lively in the ear's awareness, they each enhance the value of the other and thus form the basis for an even more complete and fulfilling experience of music.

VIII. LEVELS OF PERFECT PITCH

By now we should have a clear conception of perfect pitch as distinguished from various other musical considerations. As we have seen, color hearing is not to be confused with synesthesia or color association, nor is it in any way a reference to instrumental "tone color" or other musical definitions of the word *color*. Color hearing simply means the facility to "hear in color," which implies the ability to identify musical frequencies (pitches) by their perceived *pitch color*.

The color of a pitch could be described as a certain "quality" of sound which is peculiar to and characteristic of each musical tone. To most ears, there is apparently nothing different about one pitch from another except its "highness" or "lowness." To the color ear there is a subtle, yet distinct difference between each individual pitch—some quality which distinguishes one from the next. "Highness" or "lowness" does not enter into pitch identification—color alone is the secret of the ear's ability to know a pitch.

In the natural unfoldment of musical perception, the ear tends to proceed through several levels, or stages of development. These phases are not absolutely clear-cut, and there is a great deal of overlapping, but they do serve as a general indication of the ear's development. We will consider individually each step of progress towards fully enlivened perfect pitch.

Level One: COLOR AWARENESS

The first stage in the unfoldment of refined tonal perception is simply becoming aware of colors of pitch. The keyboard is a spectrum of sound colors which, comparatively broader in scope than the visual color spectrum, repeats in successive "tints" with every octave. Simple *color awareness* is an innocent and undeveloped stage where the ear first starts to pick up on this new abstract experience. It is similar to a child who notices visual colors but has not yet matured enough to be able to label them. And just as a child may at first confuse similar colors like red and orange until he learns to finely discriminate each color by name, the ear which is just starting to recognize color may at first "group" tones together which have a similar color sound.

Level Two: COLOR DISCRIMINATION

Whereas simple color awareness is not yet sufficiently developed to earn the label of "perfect pitch," *color discrimination* can be said to be the first true manifestation of a finely tuned ear. Color discrimination is the enlivened ability to accurately discriminate among the twelve chromatic musical colors (and their successive octave "tints"), just as one can identify the basic colors in a set of paints. This is the basic level of perfect pitch where one can identify pitches by ear alone on the instrument with which one is most familiar. Color discrimination is mature color awareness.

Level Three: REFINED COLOR DISCRIMINATION

After clearly perceiving and distinguishing the colors in the pitch spectrum of one's familiar instrument, a further advancement develops as the ear becomes sensitive to color variations *within the sphere of a single tone.* The ear at this point has become so familiar with each pitch color that it can sense to some degree the sharpness or flatness of a tone.

The sharper or flatter a tone is, the more it starts to take on the quality of its neighboring tone, just as red melts into red-orange before arriving at orange in the visual spectrum. If a flat F is sounded, the ear with *refined color discrimination* will hear it as "shaded" to some degree by the color of E and thereby notice its flatness. An ear lacking this refinement will simply hear it as an F, and if it is *very* flat may even confuse it for E.

Mozart was using his refined color discrimination to evaluate the difference between violin pitches in the story recounted earlier. One should bear in mind that Mozart was unbelievably skilled at everything he did that was musically oriented, and that it would be quite an achievement to recognize *without direct comparison* a "half a quarter tone." Yet no matter how proficient one becomes with intra-tonal discriminations, further levels of color hearing are at this stage adequately prepared for development.

Level Four: UNIVERSAL COLOR DISCRIMINATION

Pitch color perception is usually best experienced on the musical instrument with which one is most familiar. A guitarist, for example, may hear pitch colors easily on the guitar, but when listening to a flute they may somehow seem completely obscured. This surprising situation can be so striking that one may seem to have acute color hearing on his own instrument, only to appear helpless with other musical pitches. The ear may seem to have difficulty "finding" the pitch colors of tones within the different qualities of sounds from other instruments one does not practice.

This phenomenon is due to the ear's as yet underdeveloped ability to distinguish between *pitch color* and *timbre.* (Recall that timbre, or "tone color," is the textural form which a pitch takes; it is that peculiar quality of sound which gives each musical instrument its own identity, even though the same pitches are duplicated by many other instruments.) At this stage of development the ear's perception may still be somewhat "blurred," thereby lacking the focus to distinguish between "tone color" and pitch color.

When the ear learns to identify pitch color on one's familiar instrument, it is not confused by timbre because the timbre of the instrument remains constant while the pitch colors change. For example, all the tones on a piano have the timbre of a piano (obviously), yet each note on the keyboard has a different pitch color according to its vibratory frequency. When a pianist listens to the piano, his ear only has to concern itself with pitch color until faced with a different instrument's timbre. His ear could then easily become confused when exposed to an entirely new sound texture after having listened for color deep *within* the tones. The ear "surfaces" to grapple with the new overt timbre, and in so doing cannot locate the more abstract value of pitch color which lies at a subtler level of experience.

In time, however, the ear learns to universally distinguish between the "texture" of the particular instrument and the color of the pitch, which are two separate considerations. Gradually the ear is not sidetracked by different instrumental sound textures, and pitch color becomes clearly perceived through the "disguises" of many different timbres.

In advancing to this level of development, the ear naturally acquires a deeper appreciation of timbre in addition to a more refined experience of pitch color. In fact, the following equation could accurately describe this level of *universal color discrimination:*

REFINED		REFINED		UNIVERSAL
COLOR	+	TIMBRE	=	COLOR
DISCRIMINATION		DISCRIMINATION		DISCRIMINATION

Here is an example of how development of perfect pitch results in an expansion of musical awareness which in turn enlivens other aspects of musicality. The alert color ear experiences not only a keen perception of pitch color, but also a finer level of general music appreciation and sensitivity.

Level Five: SPECTRAL DISCRIMINATION

As the ear is able to clearly sense the absolute pitch color of *any* musical tone (universal color discrimination), it again can start to discriminate to some degree *in between* tones. *Spectral discrimination* is refined color discrimination when applied to any pitch spectrum on any instrument (or non-instrument). The ear becomes sensitive to the complete color spectrum of pitch in all its forms and manifestations.

Level Six: AURAL RECALL

Aural recall is the advanced achievement of the color ear. Even without actually hearing a tone, the musician with aural recall is able to *imagine* what the color of an F#, Bb, or other tone sounds like. In this way he is able to imagine and sing a tone *without hearing any tone first.* This shows that such a musician has attained a clear realization of what was formerly only an abstract perception. A true test for aural recall can be made only once in a sitting, because once any tone is heard it could be identified by its pitch color and thus indicate the location of other tones via relative pitch.

****

These progressive levels of color awareness are not completely isolated from each other. They merely indicate a basic course of the ear's ability to perceive pitch color. It is quite possible, for example, to have a very good aural recall yet not possess a high degree of spectral discrimination. However, the individual with aural recall has expanded his perception *beyond* the level of spectral discrimination, so the latter potential is already exposed and can be sharpened with greater ease.

IX. VOCAL TENSION PITCH

A pseudo "perfect pitch" sometimes develops especially among singers which relies on vocal tension in estimating pitch. By becoming familiar with one's vocal range it is possible to learn to judge a pitch by how much vocal tension is required in order to sing it. Though some singers can become fairly accurate with this, it is not reliable due to the varying conditions of the vocal mechanisms throughout the day. We have probably all experienced how much easier it is to sing in a low register upon awakening in the morning—sometimes even a minor third lower can be reached which is quite impossible during the day. Ideas of where to locate specific pitches can fluctuate in a similar manner, and are all the more confused by changes in mood, how much one has just talked or sung, or if one is tired or energetic.

Vocal tension pitch is rarely accurate enough to be mislabelled as "perfect pitch," and it does not involve pitch color discrimination. It is important for musicians who wish to develop a color ear not to become attached to this sort of pitch location. It is hard to rid oneself of this crutch, and it distracts one's focus from true color hearing.

Vocalists who are already somewhat skilled in this regard should not become concerned, however. Vocal tension pitch will not inhibit growing color discrimination if one does not use it during Color Hearing Technique practice sessions.

X. THE PRACTICALITY OF COLOR HEARING

Imagine closing your eyes, yet knowing the names of musical tones because *you hear their colors!* Imagine what the experience of music is like to the ear which has gained sensitivity to this subtle value of perception! There is a difference between the way someone with perfect pitch hears music and the way most people do. The sense of perfect pitch enriches the experience of sound in a way that no amount of theorizing can compare with.

Though a developed ear alone can never make up for technical disabilities of the performer or creative inhibitions of the composer, it forms a firm foundation of higher achievement for establishing other musical proficiencies. The ear with such an expanded musical awareness is naturally more responsive to many avenues of sound artistry. Musicians with a developed color ear tend to be the more successful and creative individuals, and sometimes even seem to enjoy music with greater vigor. Whether you are a professional musician, a performance major at a music school, or a member of your own high school music group, perfect pitch will benefit you both as a practical musician and in personal appreciation of sound.

The importance of ear-training with reference to an art which is enjoyed by *listening* cannot be overevaluated. For the serious musician, half of all music theory classes should be devoted to ear-training, and half of all ear-training sessions should be devoted to Color Hearing Technique. *When one understands how to develop perfect pitch,* it is just as easy to culture as relative pitch, and when the two are present together the ear's awareness is not doubled, but squared.

The exercises for developing a color ear are much simpler than learning intervals and are also a lot of fun. You will find that Color Hearing Technique is a different kind of challenge than relative pitch training.

The principle of increasing one's color awareness lies with the factor of *attention:* on whatever aspect of aural perception one puts the ear's attention, that aspect will tend to increase and grow in one's awareness. The perception of pitch color is a more refined and satisfying experience to the ear than one of "black and white," yet it is also a subtler experience and therefore more elusive. But if the attention is consciously and rightly directed, the ear will then have the opportunity to develop *of its own accord.*

The way to develop perfect pitch is to *listen for color.* Many musicians have attempted to gain this facility by trying to "memorize" a pitch. There is one such experiment in which Middle C would be played constantly for fifteen minutes per session to try to get it to stay in one's head.[9] Though the experimenter claimed success, this method is very roundabout and indirect, and could easily tire the ear as well as become extremely *boring.* A pitch will only stay in the mind when there is some quality about it which distinguishes it from other tones, and that quality is its *color.* Even the violinist or other musician who has apparently "memorized" a concert A due to constant orchestral tuning to this pitch has done so because he hears the *color* of A to some degree.

Color Hearing Technique must be actively *applied* in order to improve your ear, and thereby your musicianship. Do not doubt your own latent ability to develop perfect pitch just because the subject is often both misunderstood and unduly revered. Paul Hindemith wrote that his experience "time and again has proved that 'absolute pitch' can be acquired and developed," and even added that "if not, the question may be raised whether there is any musical gift at all in a mind that cannot learn to remember and compare pitches."[10] Though it is true that some musicians spontaneously develop certain skills, this does not in any way mean that others cannot achieve these skills with practice.

During college days I taught piano to three sisters—average American teenagers between the ages of 13 and 17. Before starting individual lessons we would meet as a group to study ear-training. Because these students had not been conditioned to think of perfect pitch as something extra-musical, they innocently practiced their ear-training exercises and were soon competing eagerly for first place in naming tones. No sooner would a tone be played than each would immediately name the note, making it a contest of speed rather than one of mere recognition. The point of this example is that development of musical perception is easy if one has proper direction and does not resign oneself to a lesser level of musicality.

Development of perfect pitch does not take a long time, but it does take *its own time.* Musicians progress at varying rates with different musical skills, so strict indications cannot be given for how long it will take any particular individual to develop a good color ear. The average musician, however, should be able to produce a good aural recall in a year's time or less if the forthcoming Color Hearing Technique exercises are practiced daily. This is by no means an extraordinary amount of time—think how many years it takes to become proficient on your instrument, let alone become a seasoned performer. Consider also how long one spends on other aspects of musicianship and theoretical knowledge in an effort towards greater musical fluency. The time you invest in your ear will pay high dividends for the life of your musical activities.

Color Hearing Technique is not something you will have to keep on practicing. Once established, color discrimination cannot be lost—instead you may wonder why you had not noticed pitch color previously. Enlivenment of perfect pitch requires a little time now, and later when the ear is open one just enjoys.

It is possible that your ear is so ripe in its development that you will barely even have to practice. A flutest friend back in high school insisted she did "not have perfect pitch." When I counter-insisted that she could *easily* hear the differences between the various pitch colors, she admitted that she did "seem" to, but that she still did not think she could develop "perfect" pitch. Yet in a few weeks she was explaining to other musicians how it was that she knew a pitch by ear alone, complete with her experiences of how Bb has a "softer" color than F, and how the color of F# sounds "hotter" than a "cool" Ab. It may take you a little longer than she took to develop a good color ear, but *you can do it* if, like anything else, you will just take the time.

XI. TUNE UP!

Before starting the following Color Hearing Technique exercises, it is important to make sure your instrument is always well tuned. If you are a guitarist, for example, and will only be casually playing for some friends, it would still be good to tune to concert pitch beforehand even though the guitar might otherwise be in tune. Remember that we want to cultivate a deeper perception of *particular points* within the musical spectrum (i.e., specific musical frequencies at a standard pitch level).

You can help keep your instrument in tune with a tuning fork. This familiar and practical musical tool was invented in England by trumpeter John Shore in 1711. Most music stores have been stocking them ever since at a nominal cost. A-440 is the most commonly used fork and is also the pitch to which orchestras usually tune. Other pitches are available which may be easier to use with your particular instrument, but you may have to put in a special order.

To use your fork, first grip it firmly and strike one of its arms on the heel of your palm or on your knee. Then touch the base to a wooden object. The wood will act as a sounding board to make the tone sufficiently audible. Never strike your fork on metal or anything hard, as this could dent or nick it slightly and put it out of tune.

Vocalists should regularly take time to establish proper pitch even when a piano is not available. Pitch pipes are more convenient for vocal activities. Get the best one you can—by consciously staying in tune now, you will later be able to discard your pitch pipe permanently.

String instrumentalists should learn to use *one* fork (don't get one for every ·string!) to establish a standard pitch level, and then tune each string accordingly. If your instrument is fairly new to you, you may feel it is difficult to get it sounding just right. If this happens, realize that your ear is better than you think, otherwise you would not know your instrument is not quite tuned or feel disappointed that it doesn't sound as good as you would like. Just tune up as well as you can without taking a long time and don't worry about it being "perfect." With practice and easy listening your ear will sharpen and tuning will become second nature.

Some musicians may wish to use the electronic tuning devices which have been appearing on the market. Such equipment is becoming increasingly popular, allowing fast tuning which is more accurate than a human ear—a definite plus for the performer in concert.

Some musicians have the idea that a good ear can become "ruined" by listening to pitches which are consistently sharp or flat. The truth is that if an instrument is well tuned *in itself*, yet sharp or flat to standard concert pitch, it will not "ruin" your hearing, nor make your ear "go out of tune," nor can it undermine the judgment of someone with perfect pitch. It's just that if you are newly learning to discriminate between, say, the color of F and the color of F#, it will be difficult to make a distinction if the two tones are always infringing on each other's territory. To help quickly "open up" the ear, practice only at a constant pitch level.

A musician with developed perfect pitch can never have his ear "untuned" because his ability is in hearing the complete, unbroken spectrum of pitch color. What he *calls* these colors are of little consequence. Pitch standards, in fact, were quite ambiguous in the sixteenth and seventeenth centuries, with concert A vacillating anywhere from about 373 Hz to about 567 Hz.[11] Handel had one of Shore's original tuning forks which was tuned to A-422.5; Mozart tuned his pianos to about A-422.[12] In Bach's day a concert A could often be tuned as low as 415, which would sound like Ab to the contemporary ear used to a concert A at 440. Yet if these composers were alive today, they would simply adapt by assigning their familiar note names to our newer "tinges" of pitch color (as well as possibly having all their works transposed to sound as they had intended!).*

Playing or listening to an instrument which is not in tune *in itself*, however, can have a weakening tendency towards further aural refinement. Hearing an ill-tuned instrument is like seeing through a wrong pair of glasses: perception becomes blurred. Eyes can become weakened if they cannot focus clearly; the ear can gradually start to lose its idea of what musical clarity is like and become less sensitive to harshness and dissonance if the pitches it hears are consistently not well focused. In short, one's discrimination can become lessened or dulled as a result of tuning carelessness.

Some people may wonder how the use of *equal-tempered* instruments relates to the ear's discrimination. Equal-tempered tuning is the contemporary Western way of fixing successive pitches at mathematically regular distances, exactly as described in the section entitled "Wave Frequency and Color." When spaced in this fashion, tones are not always precisely in tune with the natural harmonic overtone series, as we have mentioned.

The predecessor of tempered tuning is *just tuning*, where scale tones are adjusted to these mathematical "irregularities" and are more in accord with the overtone series. Though just tuning is theoretically the more perfect system because it produces the more consonant and natural harmonic intervals, it has a disadvantage in that an instrument so tuned can be played well only in the

---

*Concert pitch has risen over the years largely due to the clever practice of an orchestra tuning slightly sharp to give a more "brilliant" sound. Originally, in fact, the term *concert pitch* meant the brilliant pitch of an orchestra in concert. Over time, however, this effect seems to wear off and the sharper tuning tends to become a new standard, while the orchestra still desires the brilliancy of an even sharper pitch. This is an interesting trend, and seems to indicate that even the undeveloped ear naturally senses a shift in the pitch spectrum it is accustomed to.

one key to which it is tuned. The mathematics of just tuning are such that the perfect harmonic relationships established do not apply to a different key, and if other keys are attempted the sound will be *very* out of tune.

Johann Sebastian Bach formally introduced the world to equal-tempering in his *Das wohltemperierte Klavier* (1722). This volume was a progressive ideology in its day. It consisted of preludes and fugues in each of the twelve major and twelve minor keys—an effort to prove that all tonalities in an equal-tempered system are musically self-sufficient and pleasing.

Bach, who had a fully developed color ear, would not have advocated a system of tuning which would not be musically satisfactory to the ear. While it is true that just tuning is more ideal, it does not offer the wide range of harmonic possibilities available in equal-tempered tuning. Considerations along these lines are really to a large extent dependent upon personal taste and what the ear is accustomed to.

In addition to situations of tones being out of tune with each other, individual tones can also be discordant within themselves on the piano (or harpsichord). Two or three strings vibrate together for most tones on the keyboard, so if the strings for a particular tone are not focused to pitch, that tone will be blurred. Serious pianists should have tunings done two to four times per year—the natural changes of season in one's area are ideal times to tune.

It is not necessary to become a tuning fanatic. A simple tune-and-forget-it attitude will suffice. Your ear will not become hampered in acquiring pitch color discrimination with slight discrepancies in tuning. After all, you learned to identify "red" even though every "red" you see is slightly different in hue.

XII. COLOR HEARING TECHNIQUE

Color Hearing Technique is the set of progressive ear-training exercises for developing perfect pitch. These exercises culture the ear in a whole new dimension of musical perception—that of distinguishing between the various pitch colors in the sound spectrum. This enlivened potential of aural perception is the superhearing facility of color hearing.

The actual experience of pitch color is difficult to convey, but once you hear it clearly for yourself, further refinement will come very easily. The *color* of a pitch is that particular quality which is characteristic of a particular tone. Some tones sound "vibrant," some sound "soft," some could be said to sound "bright."

In describing the ability of perfect pitch, *The New Grove Dictionary of Music and Musicians* explains that "the faculty is experienced subjectively as different keys having, as it were, distinctive flavours or colours that are instantaneously recognized and never confused."[13]

The twelve chromatic tones could also be compared to twelve spices on the kitchen rack. Each has its own scent which distinguishes it from the others. If you smell rosemary, you will know it is rosemary by its own scent and not sage or thyme, even though you have not compared it to another spice.

In a similar manner, every pitch has its own particular sound which distinguishes it from other pitches. It is this unique "sound color" of a pitch which allows one to know the name of a tone.

The different octaves of a pitch could be likened to different "tints" of that same color. Every F#, for example, has the characteristic "twangy" color of an F#, no matter which octave it occurs in. The different octaves will simply determine if this color of F# is "brighter" (higher) or "darker" (lower).

In the following exercises you will be listening for these subtle differences between each musical tone within the pitch spectrum. Once your ear becomes sensitive to the color of a tone, it will be easy to label that color as F#, Ab, etc. It is never our concern to "memorize" a pitch or try to place it by how "high" or "low" it seems to be. Perfect pitch is *color* hearing, and in order to develop it we simply listen for *color*.

Once you direct your attention to a tone's color, you may be surprised at how quickly you start to pick up on this new experience. You may even wonder why you had never noticed pitch color before. If, however, for some reason you should experience an unduly "lazy" ear which refuses to sense anything different about one tone from another (except its "highness" or "lowness"), do not give up. Once you resolve to listen to the twelve chromatic pitches in order to discover their deeper sound values, it is only a matter of time before your ear becomes sensitive to them. Resolve to gently wake up your sleeping ears so that they can *really* listen!

GENERAL POINTS

The following are some general points which apply to each exercise you will be practicing:

A. *Get a partner.*

It is ideal and in fact almost essential that you find another musician who will practice these exercises with you for a few minutes each day. While drilling your partner, you will gain a great benefit just by playing and listening. A tape recorder *cannot* be used to replace the need for a partner because it not only adds a confusing "tape recorder" timbre to the tones, but it is also vital to have the sound very, very clear and "live" until you become well-accustomed to hearing pitch color. If you have difficulty finding a partner for some reason, however, much progress can still be made on your own with occasional outside help.

B. *Stay with one practice instrument.*

You may use any instrument you wish to practice these exercises, provided that you stick with it exclusively until change is advised. For convenience in drilling, the piano is probably the best instrument to use, and therefore *all exercises are geared to the keyboard.* The piano is also good because it provides a medium range of tones which many instruments do not have. You may, however, wish to use your familiar instrument (if other than piano) because pitch color may seem easier to hear on it. In this case *you may adjust any exercise in ways best suited to your particular instrument.* (For instance, if your instrument's range does not contain all practice tones called for in the exercise, you may eliminate or transpose tones not available.) Guitar is an excellent practice instrument (avoid using a 12-string guitar, however).

All references to individual tones in these exercises are in *concert pitch.* Whatever note a particular tone matches on a piano is its concert pitch, provided that the piano has been tuned so that the A above Middle C equals 440 Hz. A concert F# would therefore be a "trumpet G#" because the trumpet is pitched in Bb. If you use any instrument which is not pitched in C, you must transpose all practice tones in the exercise to match the concert pitches called for. Pitch color is not dependent on the *name* of a pitch, but rather on its *wave frequency.*

C. *Tune up!*

Be sure to keep in tune as discussed in the preceding section.

D. *Don't sing the tone!*

See section IX, "Vocal Tension Pitch." On parts of the exercise which do not require singing, be sure not to attempt to judge tones by vocal estimation. Correct practice of parts which do require singing is explained in the exercises.

E. *Take it easy. . .*

No matter how advanced you already are in music theory or ear-training, stick to just one daily practice session for the time recommended unless otherwise stated. This type of listening could tire the ear if overzealousness demands too much of it.

Repeat the same exercise daily until you have really mastered it, at which time proceed to the next exercise on the following day. Each successive exercise is quite a big step, so don't frustrate your ear by rushing and demanding too much of it all at once. Be patient with your ear and allow it to grow *naturally*. A seed will blossom into a fragrant flower in its own good time—it cannot be forced faster by excess light, water or zeal.

F. *Relative pitch considerations*

The beginning exercises may seem quite easy to those who already have a good sense of relative pitch. Because of this they may feel they are not really hearing pitch color at all, but rather are cued to the name of a tone via relative pitch. In these situations it is important that the following rule be applied throughout the practice of Color Hearing Technique:

Unless specifically recommended in the exercise, do not make a conscious effort to compare two tones to determine their interval. On the other hand, if relationships between tones are obvious to your ear, do not make any attempt to ignore these relationships or concentrate against hearing them.

This neutral, easy-going attitude is essential to correct practice of these exercises. If you can name a tone, it will not make a difference in the long run whether it was by true color hearing or relative pitch. Because they are both separate functions of aural perception, relative pitch cannot in any way interfere with the development of perfect pitch. Each successive exercise requires the ear to listen more closely to the *color* of a tone and gradually eliminates the possibility of relative pitch comparisons. More often than not, the ear with good relative pitch will discover at some point that beyond its sense of relative discrimination there awaits an already well-developed color sense which just needed to be exposed by progressively suspending relative pitch facilities.

Even if you find that you successfully pass an exercise on the basis of relative pitch *alone*, do not become concerned. Just have it in mind that your ear's main focus is *color*. The ear will naturally penetrate deeper into the experience of a pitch regardless of what else it may have been conditioned to perceive because the attention will be geared in this direction.

The factor of *attention* in the expansion of perceptual awareness is very powerful. The chief reason for the ear's lack of development has been a lack of attention to the subtle values of sound. By focusing one's attention in a particular direction, that facet of hearing can become enhanced. Though the ear has not noticed pitch color previously, all it needs to do is find the correct direction in which to listen. Having the attention geared towards color is the right start and will open the ear to this value regardless of any relative pitch considerations which may be present. When practicing these exercises, therefore, do not worry about whether you are "really" hearing pitch color or whether you are merely using relative pitch. Pitch color will become clear naturally as you take an easy attitude towards its perception and allow the ear to become increasingly sensitive of its own accord.

Relative pitch of course has a vitally important function in the well-rounded musical ear. At this time, however, we should feel that perfect pitch is *more important* to develop. The cultivation of perfect pitch will have the additional tendency to develop relative pitch anyway, because the expansion of awareness required to hear pitch color will automatically extend into other avenues of musical expertise. Most musicians with perfect pitch develop relative pitch with little or no training.

After practicing these exercises for some time, you may develop a sort of "absolute relative pitch." This phenomenon is characterized by feelings of tonal relationships even when none really exists. For instance, if played an E the ear may somehow hear it in terms of a major third above C, even though a C may not have been sounded. The ear has been conditioned for many years to hear relationships between tones and not absolute pitch color. At this point it is starting to distinguish pitch color better and is in the process of sorting out this new perception from past patterns of experience. When hearing the color of a tone, the ear may be conditioned to refer to a common way you have heard that color before, i.e., a relationship or context in which you have unconsciously appreciated that pitch sometime in the past. Soon the experience will clarify and all *associations* to that color will break off, leaving a clear perception of the pitch color alone. This situation can be characteristic of developing color discrimination, though every ear will not necessarily experience much of this phenomenon.

Instrumentalists who are not using piano for these exercises may sense obvious kinds of cues which are characteristic of their instrument (such as an open string sound which immediately gives away the name of a pitch). In these cases the same rule applies as for relative pitch considerations: simply identify the pitch while listening for color. Even with these situations your ear is becoming receptive to pitch color as you continue to practice. Soon you will be able to universally discriminate among pitch colors on *any* instrument, and your ear will make a distinction between pitch color awareness and "open string" types of awareness.

G. *Have fun!*

These simple exercises should be practiced *effortlessly* with a sense of enjoyable challenge. The expansion of musical awareness means a larger capacity for perception and artistic appreciation, so feel easy and free in your practice sessions.

COLOR HEARING TECHNIQUE EXERCISES

EXERCISE 1

Locate the octave C to C, with Middle C at the top. Starting with Low C, play the chromatic scale slowly, listening *effortlessly* to each tone. Repeat this procedure a number of times, playing up and down the keyboard at varying speeds. Listen attentively, yet easily, to this *spectrum* of pitch colors.

Within this spectrum of thirteen tones, see if you can locate any two or more tones which you feel form a "color group," that is, which have some sound quality that seems to make them more related than other tones. If you find such groups, what is it that you experience about certain tones which is similar to some tones yet different from others?

Have a large set of multicolored pencils and a sheet of paper handy. As you continue listening, try to find some abstract perceptual reason for how each tone could sound like the color of one of the pencils. Draw a color diagram of your "sound spectrum," and label each color with the note it represents.

Young students as well as adults have a lot of fun with this exercise in imaginative cross-perception. Do not underestimate the value of this drill, and don't skip it. Focusing on an activity as abstract as "listening" for visual colors gears the ear towards a new trend of sound perception. In seeking for some quality that it has not yet heard, the awareness of the ear begins to open to this newer level of color experience.

Don't become too attached to your visual/aural color associations. There can be many psychological factors rather than perceptual reasons for why you may associate a particular color to a particular tone, and there are no "right" or "wrong" responses. Also, as stated earlier, perfect pitch is not the association of visual color to tones, but rather *the perception of pitch color.* The simple but important values of this lesson are in having the ear listen for something *new* within a tone which cannot be located on the level of common perception, and in indicating a "direction" in which this new perception may be found.

The purpose of this exercise is to introduce the ear to pitch color awareness. It should take 15-20 minutes.

EXERCISE 2

Now let's examine just two tones from our color spectrum: the Eb and F# below Middle C. (It is never necessary to continue relating visual colors to tones as you did in Exercise 1.) Remember that if you are not using piano you may have to transpose notes—these are *concert pitches* of Eb and F#.

Play these tones separately many times and listen for the color of each one. It is obvious when playing them that one is pitched higher than the other. But do you hear anything else which is different about these tones?

Listen carefully some more, and soon you may start to notice the difference: the F# seems to have a sort of "vibrant" quality, whereas the Eb seems to sound "softer," more "mellow." At first you may think you hear this distinction, but then later it may elude you. Play the F# loudly and listen to its "brashness"— no matter how loudly the Eb is struck it will not sound as "twangy." It is these qualities of "vibrancy" and "softness" which are the *colors* of these two tones and which will allow you to recognize these tones just by *how they sound*.

The "vibrancy" of F# may be so immediately noticeable to you that you may wonder if there is something wrong with the piano or your ears. Rest assured that the "vibrant" quality of a concert F# is common to all instruments for any ear which is sensitive to its color. Over the years I have questioned many friends and acquaintances with perfect pitch on this point, and though many had never really thought about it until asked, all agreed this was their perception. If you can hear this distinction well, you already have a good color awareness.

It is important to note that pitch color is a function of *pitch,* and is not something that can be attributed to the actual physical mechanisms of an instrument. If you record a G or other pitch, then slow down the tape so the pitch equals F#, the pitch color will also change from the color of G to the "vibrant" color of F#.

Play F# in several different octaves. Notice how "pointed" they sound when compared to Eb played similarly. Notice that the "vibrant" color of F# and "mellow" color of Eb are always present, regardless of the octave in which these notes are played. Listen a lot with eyes closed—by cutting off the sense of sight, the attention of your hearing will increase.

Spend about five minutes comparing these two pitch colors. Then have your partner randomly play Eb and F# to see if you can determine which is which. Restrict tones used to two octaves above and two octaves below Middle C (total of four octaves). Listen carefully to the *color* of each tone, not how "high" or "low" each tone seems to be. Be sure to *let* the ear hear; do not strain trying to hear something which you may not feel sure of. Evaluate to find out if the tone sounds more like the "twangy" color of F# or the "soft" color of Eb.

After five minutes, switch and have your partner try the same drill. Practice this exercise by switching back and forth in this manner for a total of 20 minutes per session.

When you make errors in judgment, listen to the tone again. Knowing what its name is, listen again to its color. This is a vital step in your practice which should become standard procedure whenever errors are made in any exercise.

You will probably experience that soon your ear will tend to evaluate in terms of relative pitch. That is, it will know F# and Eb simply by their relationship, no matter which octave they occur in. You may then feel you are "cheating" and not really listening for pitch color at all. Don't try to concentrate against using relative pitch if this happens. Even if you know what a tone is instantly in this way, listen for its pitch color anyway. Do not become concerned that relative pitch could distract you from hearing the pitch color. At points further in these exercises there will be divergences of these two faculties, and your ear will become required to listen to pitch color more closely.

Proceed to the next exercise only after you have achieved a high degree of accuracy.

EXERCISE 3

Listen carefully to the pitch color of A for about five minutes. Compare it to the color of Eb and F# in several different octaves. The color of A may seem "bright" when compared to the "vibrant" quality of F# and the "mellow" quality of Eb. Find your own adjectives to describe these pitch colors.

It is challenging to describe a pitch color. How would you describe a visual color like red, green, or yellow? No description can really convey the experience of color unless another has had that perception. However, words and analogies are helpful in explaining the experience of pitch color because they can "hint" in such a way as to guide another ear to the same depth of perception. (Conversely, it is easier to convey experiences of audible *textures* because they are more obvious than the subtle perception of color, and most people are familiar with them. If someone exclaimed that he heard a bird with a "reedy" call, or that he had a watermelon with a "hollow" pitch when tapped, one could get a good idea of what he meant, based on one's own past experience.)

After you feel comfortable with the new color of A, include it in your listening drill. Remember to listen often with eyes closed and always with ears relaxed and receptive. Do not use tones outside the four octave limit. Switch back and forth with your partner for a total of 20 minutes per session. Proceed only when a high degree of accuracy has been established.

EXERCISE 4

Now we are ready to add C to the list, completing a diminished seventh harmonic pattern. At this point the ear will have to start relying more and more on pitch color experience. It will not be able to refer as easily to relationships among the tones because each note used in this exercise is a minor third from the next. This creates an ambiguous feeling in the ear and will cause it to start to lose any "home base" it may have had in previous exercises (i.e., before we had three tones in each octave which could have been easy to determine simply by their positions of "high," "middle," or "low"; now all the tones run together and make this kind of cue more difficult).

This exercise contains the seed form of developed perfect pitch. If you can accurately name tones across the keyboard which are spaced at intervals of a minor third, you will certainly be able to do the same with tones at a minor second as they occur in the full keyboard spectrum.

Your ability to know the name of a pitch will solidify only as your ear gradually perceives some quality which distinguishes one pitch from another. This quality is a tone's *color*. More and more these sound colors will become clear to your ear. With continued practice you will better appreciate these musical perceptions which were formerly too delicate for the ear's attention, and therefore not obvious. You may even be surprised when you find out that your particular experience of pitch color may be common to other color hearers and is not necessarily unique or private.

Although pitch color perception is certainly within the mental sphere (like all perception), it does not exist on the basis of personal idiosyncrasies the mind ascribes to pitches (as some music psychologists suppose). The visual perception of "blue" is also really only in the mind—objectively "blue" is just a wave frequency—but we experience this "mental blue" *perceptually*.

Similarly, pitch color awareness is the surfacing of a latent *perceptual awareness*. However, before you sense the abstract value of pitch color distinctly, you may seem to feel a sort of "imagination" of pitch color. This is fine—let your imagination loose. As you progress in your exercises, personal ideas of pitch color will be discarded for clearer *experience*.

In addition to 20 minutes of pitch naming between you and your partner, we will now include a pitch *singing* drill in your sessions. One individual will name one of the four tones we are using in this exercise, and the other will try to sing that tone.

Let's say your partner requests you to sing a C#. Intend to mentally hear the *color* of a C#, and then sing that pitch. *Think* the pitch before singing to avoid vocal tension pitch as much as possible (treat vocal tension considerations exactly as relative pitch considerations). Play each tone after singing to see how accurate you have been. Do this drill for two minutes before practicing your pitch naming drill. Switch with your partner for an additional two minutes.

With this addition we are now starting to cultivate aural recall of pitches. Because aural recall is so highly advanced, you may wonder why we are starting this already. You may feel at this point that pitch colors are still unclear to your *perception*, much less trying to *remember* them! Nevertheless, just the act of trying to sing these tones *consciously* (even if one were to "cheat" with relative pitch) will start to cultivate a deeper tonal experience. It is the ear's *attention* on a tone which ultimately leads to enlivenment of finer perception of that tone. It is as if the ear learns so thoroughly the superficial values of a sound that it wants to plunge within to a deeper and more refined cognition. By going after the higher developments of color hearing in this way, a perfect path is cleared for their realization.

Here is another small addition to all future practice sessions: When first starting your practice session, agree on any tone you will be using and effortlessly imagine what it sounds like. Then attempt to sing that tone without hearing another tone played. Check to see if you or your partner is more accurate. Do not become discouraged with this! Aural recall can only become firmly established after you are further along in the exercises and have developed a good sense of pitch color. If you try to remember a pitch whose color is not very clear to your ear as yet, you certainly will not be greatly accurate. But the value is this: by intending to imagine what a pitch sounds like, you are requiring the ear to expand its scope by practicing to locate the *color* of that pitch. By doing this easily and effortlessly, and *not worrying about inaccuracies*, your ear will naturally start to penetrate more and more into this newer dimension of hearing.

The total time for this exercise is about 25 minutes. Practice the pitch naming part the same way you did in the last exercise. Be sure not to sing tones on this part. Make sure to listen again for color on tones which you are incorrect in naming. Listen innocently to the *color*—don't try to memorize the "highness" or "lowness" of the pitch. Proceed when you achieve 95% accuracy on the pitch naming part.

EXERCISE 5

Note: Instrumentalists who are not using piano for practice sessions and who are unable to play chords on their instrument should skip to Exercise 7. Proceed as before, but ignore all instructions regarding aural chord analysis (part C of each exercise). Sessions will therefore be a total of about 15 minutes. Do not practice longer than this per session, but if you like you may do two sessions per day which are spaced apart by several hours.

Start your session by choosing a pitch to sing. See if you are accurate in singing that pitch.

Next, do a two-minute pitch singing drill as in Exercise 4. Switch with your partner for another two minutes.

The remaining time will be split into two ten-minute segments, ten minutes each for you and your partner. The individual at the keyboard should use this time for active listening.

Play any *two* tones you have been using in the four octave range. Sound them together and keep the keys depressed. The object for the listener is to identify the tones in order from bottom to top. Tones may be played over if they fade before they are evaluated. Do not sing any tones in this part of the exercise—*listen only.*

Now our exercises will include *aural chord analysis*, this newest drill with more than one tone at a time. Aural chord analysis is a more advanced ear-training drill which will greatly clarify your experience of pitch color. In learning to pick out a pitch color from a *group* of colors, your ear will become so sensitive and confident of its perception that it will not feel the need to search for relationships between tones in order to evaluate a pitch. While it is possible to gain color hearing through pitch naming with single tones, aural chord analysis will stabilize your perception of pitch color and ensure adequate preparation for universal color discrimination.

Playing more than one tone at a time will have a tendency to distract the ear's ability to relate previous tones heard to newer ones. This is fine, because we are not trying to *relate* tones to each other, but rather we are listening for their *color* in order to identify them.

However, when hearing two tones played together, the first thing that may register in your ear is their *interval*. It is quite possible that you may know the structure of a chord immediately upon hearing it, even though you have not yet listened for color in order to identify the actual pitches. This is also fine. When listening to more than one tone at a time, we are automatically dealing with tonal *relationships*, and it would be unnatural not to acknowledge them. In fact, when using chords, it will now be permissible to use relative pitch freely *within the context of each chord.* After identifying one tone by color, you may find it faster to determine the other tone by relationship. Relative pitch used freely in this way will actually culture a very well-rounded ear.

If your relative pitch is not so developed at this point, do not worry about it. *Color* is our primary focus. Later when you learn the relationships of these colors, it will be child's play.

The total time for this exercise is about 25 minutes. Proceed when you have achieved great accuracy with aural chord analysis.

EXERCISE 6

Instead of singing tones for two minutes each, alternate back and forth naming just *one* tone for the other to sing for a total time of four minutes. This will now be your standard "alternate pitch singing warm-up."

Next do ten minutes of aural chord analysis, except this time use three tones. Switch with your partner for another ten minutes. You may spread tones over a wide area, but stay within the four octave range. Remember not to sing tones in this part of the exercise. Name tones always from the bottom up for regularity. Listen carefully for identical notes separated by one or more octaves. Play all tones with even pressure.

After you identify one tone in the chord (by color), the others may be named more quickly by relative pitch. It is not necessary to listen to each pitch color if you can do it this way. The ear naturally hears chords in terms of tonal relationships *and* color—pitch merely fixes the color pattern of a particular chordal structure. Both color and relationship are important in chord perception, and when they are heard together the ear is even stronger than with one of these facilities considered separately.

Relative pitch without perfect pitch is like comparing shades of grey; perfect pitch without relative pitch is like seeing color without appreciation of patterns. Perfect pitch may be said to be warm, more aesthetically useful, while relative pitch may be said to be more coldly logical and theoretically practical. The two together comprise the ear of the most perceptive musicians—an ear which is worth more than all the music theory courses one could take.

For some individuals it may be necessary to listen separately to each tone within the chord (listening for color while all three tones are continuously held down). Have the chord played over when the sound runs out and you need more time. Do not feel you *must* make any effort towards hearing relationships. Our main focus is *color*, which is the deeper part of aural perception. An ear with the broad foundation of color perception will have no trouble evaluating relationships.

Proceed only when you have achieved 95% accuracy with aural chord analysis.

EXERCISE 7

The schedule now will be:

(a)   4 minutes alternate pitch singing (see Exercise 6). (Don't forget to choose and sing a pitch before starting your exercise.)
(b)   5 minutes pitch naming with C, C#, Eb, F# and A; switch with partner.
(c)   5 minutes aural chord analysis using two and three note chords; switch with partner.

Note the addition of C# to your list. At your first session spend an additional few minutes listening to the color of C# within the four octave range. Discuss its color in comparison to other colors. What tone does C# sound most like to your ear? (Do you notice a "vibrant" quality similar to F#?)

Now that C# is in your list, we again have a kind of irregularity which could give easy cues in pitch naming. This is no concern, however. Just have the attention on color. By now color awareness is starting to become established.

When practicing aural chord analysis, do not tell your partner when you are playing two notes or three notes. It is up to the listener to figure this out.

Total time for this exercise is about 25 minutes. Proceed when you have achieved 95% accuracy on part (b), pitch naming with single tones.

EXERCISE 8

Add E to your list of tones, using the same schedule as Exercise 7. Proceed with succeeding exercises when you achieve 95% accuracy with part (b) and you feel the new tone has become established in your ear.

EXERCISE 9

Add G to your list.

EXERCISE 10

Add Bb. At this point do aural chord analysis with two, three and four notes per chord.

EXERCISE 11

Add D.

EXERCISE 12

Add F. If you wish you may spend longer amounts of time per session, but no more than about 30-35 minutes. *(Instrumentalists not practicing aural chord analysis may go up to 20 minutes per session if they wish.)*

EXERCISE 13

Add Ab.

EXERCISE 14

Add B. Proceed only after achieving a high degree of accuracy with aural chord analysis using three note chords.

Note: Instrumentalists who have not been practicing aural chord analysis should change from their instrument to piano or guitar and return to Exercise 7 upon mastery of this exercise. Having gained color discrimination, this procedure will enable further ear-training with chords while simultaneously developing universal color discrimination. Aural chord analysis is very different from pitch naming with single tones and will secure much greater clarity of pitch color recognition. Having become sensitive to colors on your familiar instrument, your ear will now learn to pick them out from groups of tones.

For parts (a) and (b) of each exercise, continue to use all chromatic tones, but for aural chord analysis (part c) use only the tones included in the exercise. Continue again through the exercises as before, but study the discussion of universal color discrimination in Exercise 18, especially paragraph four. Listen often to pitch colors on your familiar instrument and compare them to pitch colors on other instruments. Notice that different instrumental _textures_ can still exhibit the same _colors_.

EXERCISE 15

All chromatic tones within the four octave range have now been included in your practice. If you have been proceeding at a moderate rate (not rushing to get to the next exercise), that abstract sense of color awareness has now been cultured to the point where we can say it has become *color discrimination*. You obviously hear a spectrum of colors which you have learned to name, otherwise you would not be able to proceed to this exercise. And your success in aural chord analysis is proof that no matter where a tone lies in a musical structure, you are able to pick it out by its color.

The focus now is to expand your color discrimination to include all the various "tints" of a tone in each octave. You are familiar at this point with how each tone sounds the same in all octaves, except that each octave seems to be a different "shade" of that same color. To distinguish between these octaves we will label each tone with a unique name. There are many "accepted" but rather confusing ways of identifying concert pitches, yet there is really no absolutely standard way of doing this. The easiest and probably best way is to simply number consecutively each of the twelve chromatic tones from bottom to top. Thus the lowest tones on the keyboard are A1, Bb1, B1, etc. Middle C would be C4. *(Note: Instrumentalists using guitar for practice sessions can adopt a system of labelling notes which correlates to the piano. The lowest guitar tone, for instance, would be E2. On other instruments not pitched in C, use the number of the identical pitch on the piano. For example, Bb5 on the piano would be C5 on a Bb clarinet.)*

Practice this exercise exactly as the last, but this time learn the specific name of each tone you have been using.

A good technique for the pitch naming drill is to play at a fast, constant speed to see how quickly you or your partner can perceive and name the tones. If there is one that you are unsure of or name incorrectly, just skip it and continue with an even rhythm of playing and naming. It is not necessary to name which octave the tone is in when practicing speed. This technique helps sharpen perceptual alertness and can be practiced from time to time in addition to the regular parts of this exercise.

How is your aural recall doing? By now your ear perceives pitch colors well enough to start inwardly remembering them. This is trickier than one might suspect, however. You will probably for some time be able to name a tone you hear very easily, yet when you try to think of it mentally you may not be able to locate the pitch. Yet you certainly have some memory of the tone.

The reason is this: Memory is a much finer aspect of the mind than perception. Perception is right on the surface of the mind—the most obvious, most concrete aspect of awareness. Memory is a very delicate aspect of the mind—a mere *impression* of your previous perception. Just as pitch color was once abstract to your ear (perception), it will now probably be abstract to your memory. In time, however, you will remember more clearly, and any pitch will come at will by remembering its color sound.

You are now ready for an advanced method to help you remember the pitch color of a tone. The best way to imagine what a tone sounds like is to imagine the color sound of the major chord which uses that tone as its keynote. For example, if your partner requests that you sing an A, effortlessly try to imagine what an A major chord would sound like. Then after attempting to sing an A, have your partner play an A major chord using the notes A, C#, E and A in close position. After practicing in this way for some time, you will learn to quickly hear the different color patterns of major chords. This will greatly aid your color memory because you will hear the *color* of a pitch as different from other pitches *and also* the *color pattern* of a chord as different from other chords. Then you may find that it is actually easier to mentally hear a tone by imagining the color of its major chord.

When errors are made in this part of your exercise, you have not yet remembered the pitch colors clearly enough. Listen carefully to the chord built on that note. Then, without playing, hear this chordal color pattern in your head. Sing the keynote. In this way your perception will continue to develop and your memory will become clear.

Pitch singing in this manner is now an extremely important part of your exercise. In fact, when practicing aural chord analysis, it would be good to use these same major chords from time to time so that you also get used to identifying by ear these chords which you are practicing to remember.

EXERCISE 16

Continue as before, but add one octave in either direction. Play single tones frequently in these extremes. Chord tones may be spread out as far as you'd like. Don't strain with chords completely in an extreme low register; they will be so muddy that even Mozart might have difficulty with them! Complete chords *should* be used in the extreme *upper* register.

EXERCISE 17

Add the remaining tones of the keyboard. These tones will prove to be "ear teasers" for awhile, but with practice you can master even those dark bottom few tones.

EXERCISE 18

You have now cultured your ear to a high degree of color discrimination. The colors you hear for each tone are absolutely constant functions of pitch. This means that any identical pitch has the same color on *any* instrument (or *non*-instrument!). Yet your ear may experience confusion in perceiving these identical colors within the infinitely different varieties of timbre.

The aim now is to broaden your pitch color discrimination to include color perception of *any* pitch you hear, whether it be your familiar instrument, an "unfamiliar" instrument, or the grandfather clock striking the hour. There are many drills you can use to "universalize" your color perception.

One way is to go to a piano, open it up, and *pluck* the strings inside. Individual tones and whole chords can be played in this manner, giving a very different sound for your ear to grapple with. After determining the pitches, you can check yourself by playing tones in the usual way.

At first pitch colors may seem heavily veiled within the context of different timbres. When you make an error in pitch evaluation, listen again to the tone. If, for example, you missed a G#, listen again and notice that even when the musical tone of another instrument sounds "different," it still contains the *color* of G#. By repeatedly listening for your familiar perception of color in tones which seem to veil that color, your ear will gradually make the distinction between pitch color and timbre.

Listen closely to all pitches you hear. Have friends with various instruments sit with you to get used to the sound of pitch color on their instruments. Listen for the key in which songs and pieces are played on the radio, at concerts, and on records. Listen to *any* sound you hear: church bells, whistles, horns, glasses of water, etc. A friend of mine had a Siamese cat that meowed on a Bb! Don't be afraid to check your judgments by ironically carrying a tuning fork. As your ear continues to sharpen, you will start to gain great confidence in your judgments and soon will not feel the need to check yourself. By consciously listening in this way, your ear will not only refine its color discrimination, but it will also become increasingly appreciative of the different qualities of timbre.

It is not necessary to concern yourself with naming the octave of a pitch when listening to many different timbres. You will probably find that naming octaves other than on your familiar instrument is trickier than you might suspect, and that this in itself could entail another exercise if you so desired.

Developing universal color discrimination is a very advanced level of musical perception. The color hearing you had acquired even back in Exercise 15 was very discriminative and therefore earned the label of "perfect pitch." Since then, however, your ear has opened in many more ways. You can see that there is really no limit to the possible expansion of musical awareness.

As far as future practice is concerned, you are now on your own. You may find that even *without* practice your pitch will continue to develop simply because you took the time to set your ear listening in a direction it had not taken previously. You will find as you discriminate more easily between universal varieties of pitch that *spectral discrimination* (judging the sharpness or flatness of any tone) will also naturally grow.

The most important exercise to practice at this point is pitch singing. When you can readily remember a tone without even hearing it first, you certainly will know it whenever it is heard.

Consider yourself to have mastered Color Hearing Technique when you achieve 95% accuracy in both single tone pitch naming on any instrument (universal color discrimination) and pitch singing (aural recall).

XIII. EAR TEASERS FOR SUPER EARS

During high school days, one of my very best friends and I used to have fun thinking up all sorts of outrageous hearing tests for each other. Here are some of them for you and your partner to experiment with. Do not feel that they are "impossible," because they aren't. And they can be as much fun in trying to outwit the other as they are effective in sharpening your already clear color ear.

- Locate an entire octave of diatonic (scale) tones. Leave one out and play all the others simultaneously in one tone cluster. Have your partner name the missing tone. Repeat, using scales in different keys. Hint: First listen for and identify the keynote of the scale being played. Then "climb" the scale with your ear while listening for a "gap" in the tones.

- Play all but one of eight consecutive whole-tone scale tones together in one tone cluster. Name the missing tone.

- Play five to ten tones in any kind of chord pattern. Name all tones in order from bottom to top. This is tricky because sometimes a few tones may be difficult to hear. Be sure the player strikes the chord in a very even manner. Also, because your ear is so sharp, you may hear *overtones* and confuse them for actual notes. Watch for this! This is an even better exercise if all the intervals are half and whole tones.

- Play all but one of seven to ten consecutive chromatic tones together in one tone cluster. Name the missing note as well as the low and high tones of the series.

- Find a partner who plays the same instrument that you play. One individual plays scales starting in any key, moving up to successive chromatic keys upon completion of each scale, while the other tries to locate where the tones are so as to join in playing exactly together. The goal is to be sure on the first attempt so that tones played in error do not cue the ear via relative pitch. This same drill can be practiced with chromatic scales and arpeggios, and on piano octaves of any pattern.

- Listen to some modern progressive music. Choose any note and listen for it somewhere in the music. Go up the chromatic scale until you have listened for and picked out each tone.

- Attempt to tune a guitar or other string instrument to concert pitch by ear alone. Check yourself with a tuning fork or piano. This exercise will greatly improve spectral discrimination.

- Using any musical score, take a melodic line and *slowly* listen *mentally* to the pitch color of each tone. Even if you can fluently read the score, go very slowly and listen closely to the pitch in your mind until you perceive its *color*. This exercise will make you a master of aural recall.

XIV. PERFECT PITCH, MUSIC AND HIGHER CONSCIOUSNESS

Every musician experiences that the power and influence of organized sound is vast. Sound waves can create anything from a single tone to a rich symphony or, at another extreme, can shatter glass or crumble the walls of Jericho. Experiments have shown that certain sounds stimulate plant growth while others inhibit life.[14] Plato discussed the characteristic effects of the Greek musical modes on the human psyche. Early Christian musicology recognized these influences and responded by extracting only those modes leading to edification. The traditional Jewish modes "were an esoteric secret of the priestly class" designed to "attune the human soul to the various emotions expressed in the Scriptures and post-Biblical poetry of Judaism."[15] The great sages of ancient India proclaimed that the *entire universe* is a manifestation of one basic vibration which emanates from eternal silence, and that anything can be effected in life by proper use of specific sound patterns, or *mantras*.

As the language of the heart, music possesses the peculiar ability to encode emotions and feelings within its structure and to culture those characteristics in the heart of the listener. Whatever the music is, whatever qualities it expresses, these are rendered once again new, alive and vital in the listener's awareness, just as sympathetic vibrations are induced in one string by the identical vibrations of another. The coherent artistry of the composer's imagination becomes transformed into musical experience, and thereby infuses that same coherence into the listener's awareness. It is this transmission of inner harmony that at once captivates the listener and at the same time cultures an inner enrichment.

The oldest music on earth is the hymns of the *Veda*, a system of sacred chant cognized by the ancient *rishis* of India that records a comprehensive technology for the development of consciousness. The Vedic tradition incorporates a complete analysis of life to aid human development, yet the verbal significance of the hymns are superficial to their real purpose. Their deeper value lies in the *rhythm* and *sound* of the hymns, which in themselves are said to encode the highest knowledge available to man.[16]

In tracing the development of musical awareness, it seems to be the ear's aspiration to gradually learn to break down and identify the different levels of a sound until it arrives perceptually at the essential basis of that sound. Though every ear is presented with all the components of musical experience, this in itself does not ensure that the finer aspects of music will be consciously appreciated without training. A progression of developing aural awareness can be traced from the level of non-musicality to the most highly refined musical perception (see Figure 5). When viewed in this light, perfect pitch is a higher level of perceptual alertness than is commonly realized which itself precedes even fuller values of musical experience.

To illustrate, let's take a simple chord composed of the notes C, E and G, and trace the perception of this chord through the successive levels of musical awareness described in Figure 5.

The non-musical ear will of course hear each of these three tones when played in a chord, but it will not be able to separate individual tones from the overall sound. What registers in the completely non-musical ear is just the overall sound of the chord, without appreciation of any other aspect of it.

The average individual naturally possesses an ear more musically appreciative and will be able to hear that there are actually three tones which make up this somewhat "happy" sound, thereby sensing an intrinsic emotional reaction to what is really only a set of specific wave frequencies. Further refinement of perception is realized by the musician with relative pitch, who will explain that the structure of the chord is such that the intervals from the bottom note are a major third and a perfect fifth, which therefore form a major triad. The musician with perfect pitch will place the tones exactly as C, E and G, and observe that this particular pattern forms a unique pitch color scheme. The rare musician whose awareness can *transcend* these outward levels of perception will cognize the silence of his own awareness as being intimately connected with the perception of these musical tones. It is this latter experience which reveals to oneself the essential unity of the musician and his art.

The development of musical awareness can thus be traced from the simplest state of hearing, through various stages of sound cognition, to the profound basis of one's own inner awareness. The true Master of Music is not one who has earned such an academic degree, but rather the musician who has refined his perception sufficiently to be able to comprehend the source, course, and goal of musical processes.

The potential of aural perception is vast. Patanjali, the ancient sage who organized the system of yoga, has described various *siddhis*, or "perfections of consciousness" in his *Yoga Sutras*. By practicing a technique known as *samyama*, certain abilities can be mastered which, like perfect pitch, may appear as supernormal to the average individual. With reference to hearing, Patanjali says it is possible to culture abilities to comprehend the sounds of all creatures, hear things clearly at extreme distances, and perceive the subtle sounds of creation which cannot be heard with our physical ears.

This potential of the ear is mentioned numerous times in many ancient writings. The fully enlightened man is said to possess not only a profound cognition of the nature of life, but also a perceptual scope developed far beyond common experience. "With that clear Heavenly Ear surpassing the ear of men, he hears sounds both human and celestial, whether far or near."[17] Divine hearing is said to be one of the superknowledges which anyone can attain simply by expanding one's awareness and cultivating pure consciousness.

The fully developed musician is a master of coherent sound. He knows how to structure a musical phrase so that maximum integration occurs between the sense of hearing and the heart of the listener. He is proficient at re-energizing a phrase during his performance to ensure responsive penetration into the listener's awareness. He is a deep thinker whose feelings run deep and spill freely into his music.

The greatness and strength of a musician are ultimately found with his depth of inner awareness, and the degree to which he can express this outwardly. In *Greatness in Music*, Alfred Einstein wrote that "greatness means the construction of an inner world, and the communication of this inner world to the physical world of humanity."[18] The inspirational impact of a musician's art is dependent upon his own personal development—the cultivation of his own perception and consciousness. This is the fundamental resource of musicianship.

The art of music has always been imbibed with the ability to pass beyond mere theory or philosophy; music has the capability to express the most delicate and highest values of human existence. The ear of every man has been given this precious gift of musical awareness—the potential to unfold, appreciate, and enjoy the totality of all that can possibly be heard.

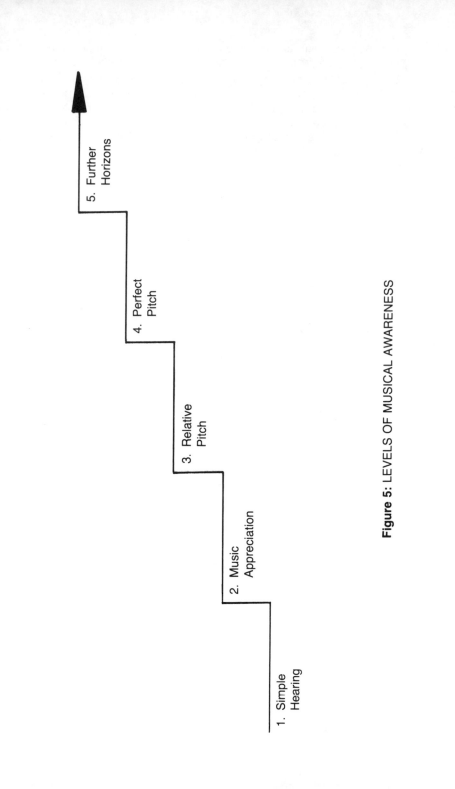

Figure 5: LEVELS OF MUSICAL AWARENESS

1. Simple Hearing

a. Hearing in terms of "sound" (non-musical appreciation)
b. Perceptual hearing
c. What the music sounds like
d. Tonal sounds
e. Level of non-musicality

2. Music Appreciation

a. Common musical sense
b. Conceptual hearing
c. What effects the music has
d. Interpretation
e. Level of the music student

3. Relative Pitch

a. Skills derived through appreciation of musical relationships and structures
b. Horizontal hearing
c. How the music was constructed
d. Composition
e. Level of the musician

4. Perfect Pitch

a. Color hearing (skills derived through appreciation of individual music building blocks)
b. Vertical hearing
c. What the music is made from
d. Color
e. Level of the artist

5. Further Horizons

a. Celestial perception (skills derived through appreciation of one's own awareness as the essential aspect of musical experience)
b. Inner hearing
c. Where the music is based
d. Silent awareness
e. Level of the music master

NOTES

1. Percy A. Scholes, *The Oxford Companion to Music* (London: Oxford University Press, 1956), p. 2.
2. John Booth Davies, *The Psychology of Music* (Stanford: Stanford University Press, 1978), p. 130.
3. A. Bachem, "Absolute Pitch," *Journal of the Acoustical Society of America*, 27, No. 6 (November 1955), 1185.
4. Paramahansa Yogananda, *Autobiography of a Yogi* (Los Angeles: Self-Realization Fellowship, 1974), p. 183.
5. Scholes, p. 204.
6. Faber Birren, *Color Psychology and Color Therapy* (New Hyde Park, New York: University Books, Inc., 1961), p. 163.
7. Scholes, p. 202.
8. "Absolute Pitch," *The New Grove Dictionary of Music and Musicians* (London: Macmillan Publishers Limited, 1980).
9. H. K. Mull, "The Acquisition of Absoute Pitch," *American Journal of Psychology*, 36 (1925), 469-493.
10. Paul Hindemith, *Elementary Training for Musicians* (London: Schott and Co., Ltd., 1946), pp. 206, 207.
11. William L. Sumner, "A History of Musical Pitch," *Hinrichsen's Musical Yearbook* (London: Hinrichsen's Edition Ltd., 1952), VII, pp. 237-238.
12. *Ibid. Also* Scholes, p. 814.
13. "Absolute Pitch," *The New Grove Dictionary of Music and Musicians.*
14. Peter Thompkins and Christopher Bird. *The Secret Life of Plants* (New York: Harper and Row, 1973), pp. 145-162.
15. Eric Werner, "The Music of Post-Biblical Judaism," *The New Oxford History of Music* (London: Oxford University Press, 1966), pp. 322-323.
16. Maharishi Mahesh Yogi, lecture at the International Course on Vedic Science, Indian Express Building, New Delhi, India, December, 1980.
17. *Samannaphala-sutta* (tr. Rhys Davids) as quoted in: Mircea Eliade, *Yoga, Immortality and Freedom* (Princeton: Princeton University Press, 1969), p. 178.
18. Alfred Einstein, *Greatness in Music* (New York: Oxford University Press, 1941), p. 163.